Practical
Pre-School

Planning
for Learning
through

Rachel Sparks Linfield and Penny Coltman

Illustrated by Cathy Hughes

Contents

Published by Step Forward Publishing Limited
The Coach House, Cross Road, Leamington Spa CV32 5PB   Tel: 01926 420046
© Step Forward Publishing Limited 2001

Planning for Learning through Winter   ISBN: 1-902438-45-0

MAKING PLANS

WHY PLAN?

The purpose of planning is to make sure that all children enjoy a broad and balanced curriculum. All planning should be useful. Plans are working documents which you spend time preparing, but which should later repay your efforts. Try to be concise. This will help you in finding information quickly when you need it.

LONG-TERM PLANS

Preparing a long-term plan, which maps out the curriculum during a year or even two, will help you to ensure that you are providing a variety of activities and are meeting the statutory requirements of the *Curriculum Guidance for the Foundation Stage* (2000).

Your long-term plan need not be detailed. Divide the time period over which you are planning into fairly equal sections, such as half terms. Choose a topic for each section. Young children benefit from making links between the new ideas they encounter so as you select each topic, think about the time of year in which you plan to do it. A topic about minibeasts will not be very successful in November!

Although each topic will address all the learning areas, some could focus on a specific area. For example, a topic on Spring would lend itself well to activities relating to knowledge and understanding of the living world. Another topic might particularly encourage the appreciation of stories. Try to make sure that you provide a variety of topics in your long-term plans.

Autumn 1	All about me
Autumn 2	Winter/Christmas
Spring 1	People who help us
Spring 2	Nursery rhymes
Summer 1	Toys
Summer 2	Minibeasts

MEDIUM-TERM PLANS

Medium-term plans will outline the contents of a topic in a little more detail. One way to start this process is by brainstorming on a large piece of paper. Work with your team writing down all the activities you can think of which are relevant to the topic. As you do this it may become clear that some activities go well together. Think about dividing them into themes. The topic of Winter, for example, has themes such as 'Snow', 'Ice' and 'Winter food'.

At this stage it is helpful to make a chart. Write the theme ideas down the side of the chart and put a different area of learning at the top of each column. Now you can insert your brainstormed ideas and will quickly see where there are gaps. As you complete the chart take account of children's earlier experiences and provide opportunities for them to progress.

Refer back to the *Curriculum Guidance for the Foundation Stage* and check that you have addressed as many different aspects of it as you can. Once all your medium-term plans are complete make sure that there are no neglected areas.

MAKING PLANS

DAY-TO-DAY PLANS

The plans you make for each day will outline aspects such as:

- resources needed;
- the way in which you might introduce activities;
- the organisation of adult help;
- size of the group;
- timing.

Identify the learning which each activity is intended to promote. Make a note of any assessments or observations that you are likely to carry out. On your plans make notes of which activities were particularly successful, or any changes you would make another time.

A FINAL NOTE

Planning should be seen as flexible. Not all groups meet every day, and not all children attend every day. Any part of the plans in this book can be used independently, stretched over a longer period or condensed to meet the needs of any group. You will almost certainly adapt the activities as children respond to them in different ways and bring their own ideas, interests and enthusiasms. Be prepared to be flexible over timing as some ideas prove more popular than others. The important thing is to ensure that the children are provided with a varied and enjoyable curriculum which meets their individual developing needs.

USING THE BOOK

To use this book:

- Collect or prepare suggested resources as listed on page 21.
- Read the section which outlines links to the Early Learning Goals (pages 4 - 7) and explains the rationale for the topic of Winter.
- For each weekly theme two activities are described in detail as examples to help you in your planning and preparation. Key vocabulary, questions and learning opportunities are identified. Many other ideas are suggested for each subject area. You can expand these in the same way.

- The skills chart on page 23 will help you to see at a glance which aspects of children's development are being addressed as a focus each week.
- As children take part in the Winter topic activities, their learning will progress. 'Collecting evidence' on page 22 explains how you might monitor children's achievements.
- Find out on page 20 how the topic can be brought together in a grand finale involving parents, children and friends.

- There is additional material to support the working partnership of families and children in the form of a 'Home links' page, and a photocopiable 'Parent's page' found at the back of the book.

It is important to appreciate that the ideas presented in this book will only be a part of your planning. Many activities which will be taking place as routine in your group may not be mentioned. For example, it is assumed that sand, dough, water, puzzles, floor toys and large scale apparatus are part of the ongoing pre-school experience. Many groups will also be able to provide access to computers and other aspects of information and communication technology. Role play areas, stories, rhymes and singing, and group discussion times are similarly assumed to be happening each week although they may not be a focus for described activities.

USING THE EARLY LEARNING GOALS

Having decided on your topic and made your medium-term plans you can use the Early Learning Goals to highlight the key learning opportunities your activities will address. The goals are split into six areas: Personal, Social and Emotional Development, Communication, Language and Literacy, Mathematical Development, Knowledge and Understanding of the World, Physical Development and Creative Development. Do not expect each of your topics to cover every goal but your long-term plans should allow for every child to work towards all of the goals.

The following section highlights parts of the *Curriculum Guidance for the Foundation Stage* (2000) in point form to show what children are expected to be able to do in each area of learning by the time they enter Year 1. These points will be used throughout this book to show how activities for a topic on Winter link to these expectations. For example, Personal, Social and Emotional Development point 8 is 'work as part of a group or class taking turns'. Activities suggested which provide the opportunity for children to do this will have the reference PS8. This will enable you to see which parts of the Early Learning Goals are covered in a given week and plan for areas to be revisited and developed.

In addition you can ensure that activities offer variety in the outcomes to be encountered. Often a similar activity may be carried out to achieve different learning outcomes. For example, when going on a walk to detect signs of Winter children will be able to develop aspects of Knowledge and Understanding of the World. At the same time, however, they can also be encouraged to work as a group, to explore new learning and to treat living things and the environment with care. In this way children will at the same time be furthering their Personal, Social and Emotional Development. It is important therefore that activities have clearly defined learning outcomes so that these may be emphasised during the activity and for recording purposes.

PERSONAL, SOCIAL AND EMOTIONAL DEVELOPMENT (PS)

This area of learning covers important aspects of development which affect the way children learn, behave and relate to others.

By the end of the Foundation Stage, most children will:

PS1   continue to be interested, excited and motivated to learn

PS2   be confident to try activities, initiate ideas and speak in a familiar group

PS3   maintain attention, concentrate and sit quietly when appropriate

PS4   have a developing awareness of their own needs, views and feelings and be sensitive to the needs, views and feelings of others

PS5   have a developing respect for their own cultures and beliefs and those of other people

PS6   respond to significant experiences, showing a range of feelings when appropriate

PS7   form good relationships with peers and adults

PS8   work as part of a group or class taking turns and sharing fairly; understanding that there need to be agreed values and codes of behaviour for groups of people, including adults and children, to work harmoniously

PS9   understand what is right, what is wrong and why

PS10   dress and undress independently and manage their own personal hygiene

PS11   select and use activities and resources independently

PS12   consider the consequences of their words and actions for themselves and others

PS13   understand that people have different needs, views, cultures and beliefs which need to be treated with respect

PS14   understand that they can expect others to treat their needs, views, cultures and beliefs with respect

The topic of Winter provides valuable opportunities for children to treat living things properly and to show concern for their local environment. Through thinking of birds and feeding them during the Winter months children will be sensitive to the needs of others. Many of the areas outlined above will be covered on an almost incidental basis as children carry out the activities described for the other areas of learning. For example, when children play games and join in with number rhymes they will also be learning to play collaboratively.

COMMUNICATION, LANGUAGE AND LITERACY (L)

The objectives set out in the *National Literacy Strategy: Framework for Teaching* for the reception year are in line with these goals. By the end of the Foundation Stage, most children will be able to:

L1   enjoy listening to and using spoken and written language and readily turn to it in their play and learning

L2   explore and experiment with sounds, words and texts

L3   listen with enjoyment and respond to stories, songs and other music, rhymes and poems and make up their own stories, songs, rhymes and poems

L4   use language to imagine and recreate roles and experiences

L5   use talk to organise, sequence and clarify thinking, ideas, feelings and events

L6   sustain attentive listening, responding to what they have heard by relevant comments, questions or actions

L7   interact with others, negotiating plans and activities and taking turns in conversation

L8   extend their vocabulary, exploring the meaning and sounds of new words

L9   retell narratives in the correct sequence, drawing on language patterns of stories

L10   speak clearly and audibly with confidence and control and show awareness of the listener, for example by their use of conventions such as greetings, 'please' and 'thank you'

L11   hear and say initial and final sounds in words and short vowel sounds within words

L12   link sounds to letters, naming and sounding the letters of the alphabet

L13   read a range of familiar and common words and simple sentences independently

L14   show an understanding of the elements of stories, such as main character, sequence of events, and openings and how information can be found in non-fiction texts to answer questions about where, who, why and how

L15   know that print carries meaning and, in English, is read from left to right and top to bottom

L16   attempt writing for various purposes, using features of different forms such as lists, stories and instructions

L17   write their own names and other things such as labels and captions and begin to form simple sentences, sometimes using punctuation

L18   use their phonic knowledge to write simple regular words and make phonetically plausible attempts at more complex words

L19   use a pencil and hold it effectively to form recognisable letters, most of which are correctly formed

The activities suggested for the topic of Winter provide the opportunity for children to respond to a variety of imaginative situations including stories and role play. The writing of labels for displays and the Winter menus will help children to develop their early writing skills which may start with pictures and progress to beginning to form letters. Throughout all the activities children will be encouraged to communicate fluently and with meaning.

MATHEMATICAL DEVELOPMENT (M)

The key objectives in the *National Numeracy Strategy: Framework for Teaching* for the reception year are in line with these goals. By the end of the Foundation Stage, most children will be able to:

M1   say and use number names in order in familiar contexts

M2   count reliably up to ten everyday objects

M3   recognise numerals 1 to 9

M4   use language such as 'more' or 'less' to compare two numbers

M5   in practical activities and discussion begin to use the vocabulary involved in adding and subtracting

M6   find one more or one less than a number from one to ten.

M7   begin to relate addition to combining two groups of objects and subtraction to 'taking away'

M8   talk about, recognise and recreate simple patterns

M9   use language such as 'circle' or 'bigger' to describe the shape and size of solids and flat shapes

M10   use everyday words to describe position

M11   use developing mathematical ideas and methods to solve practical problems

M12   use language such as 'greater', 'smaller', 'heavier' or 'lighter' to compare quantities

As children carry out the activities in this topic, seasonal artefacts, songs and images are used to introduce and reinforce the fundamental counting skills of number awareness and one to one matching. The development of mathematical vocabulary is a priority and the importance of encouraging children to talk about their first-hand experience is emphasised throughout the topic. Problem-solving, measurement and pattern are encountered in wintry contexts.

KNOWLEDGE AND UNDERSTANDING OF THE WORLD (K)

By the end of the Foundation Stage most children will be able to:

K1   investigate objects and materials by using all of their senses as appropriate

K2   find out about, and identify, some features of living things, objects and events they observe

K3   look closely at similarities, differences, patterns and change

K4   ask questions about why things happen and how things work

K5   build and construct with a wide range of objects, selecting appropriate resources and adapting their work where necessary

K6   select the tools and techniques they need to shape, assemble and join materials they are using

K7   find out about and identify the uses of everyday technology and use information and communication technology and programmable toys to support their learning

K8   find out about past and present events in their own lives, and in those of their families and other people they know

K9   observe, find out about and identify features in the place they live and the natural world

K10   begin to know about their own cultures and beliefs and those of other people

K11   find out about their environment, and talk about those features they like and dislike

The topic of Winter provides ample opportunity for children to explore and recognise features of living things. Activities which relate to both the natural and the made world will encourage children to look at similarities and differences. Observation is a strong element of the topic with children watching birds feeding, changes occurring through cooking and ice melting. Throughout all the activities children should be given the chance to talk about their experiences and to ask questions.

PHYSICAL DEVELOPMENT (PD)

By the end of the Foundation Stage most children will be able to:

PD1   move with confidence, imagination and in safety

PD2   move with control and coordination

PD3   show awareness of space, of themselves and of others

PD4   recognise the importance of keeping healthy and those things which contribute to this

PD5   recognise the changes that happen to their bodies when they are active

PD6   use a range of small and large equipment

PD7   travel around, under, over and through balancing and climbing equipment

PD8   handle tools, objects, construction and malleable materials safely and with increasing control

Activities involving mime and dance are used thematically to support children's developing abilities to express their ideas and feelings through movement. Gross motor skills are also encouraged through games and the use of large apparatus. As children manipulate materials in a variety of 'making' activities they will develop fine muscle control and co-ordination.

CREATIVE DEVELOPMENT (C)

By the end of the Foundation Stage, most children will be able to:

C1   explore colour, texture, shape, form and space in two or three dimensions

C2   recognise and explore how sounds can be changed, sing simple songs from memory, recognise repeated sounds and sound patterns and match movements to music

C3   respond in a variety of ways to what they see, hear, smell, touch and feel

C4   use their imagination in art and design, music, dance, imaginative and role play and stories

C5   express and communicate their ideas, thoughts and feelings by using a widening range of materials, suitable tools, imaginative and role play, movement, designing and making, and a variety of songs and musical instruments

During this topic children will experience working with a variety of materials as they make models, prepare seasonal edible treats and explore a range of art and craft activities. Close observation is encouraged with children recording their ideas using a variety of media. Children will develop awareness of shape, form and space as they handle equipment, cut, join and explore materials. Ideas are expressed through a variety of media including paint, chalks and collage.

Week 1
DETECTING WINTER

PERSONAL, SOCIAL AND EMOTIONAL DEVELOPMENT

- Look at a large picture of a Winter scene (trees with no leaves, people dressed in warm clothes, people skiing and skating). Discuss what children like to do in Winter. Talk about how they feel in the Winter. What are their favourite activities? What do they do when it is dark in the evenings and they cannot play outside? (PS2, 3, 4)

- Discuss festivals which children in the group celebrate during Winter. Invite parents to come and talk to children about the celebrations. (PS5)

COMMUNICATION, LANGUAGE AND LITERACY

- Make a collaborative big book about Winter (see activity opposite). (L18, 19)

MATHEMATICAL DEVELOPMENT

- Choose a Winter theme for a display to reinforce awareness of a chosen number. For example if the number chosen is five, make a display showing the numeral 5, and a variety of collections of five objects: snowflakes, snowmen, winter hats, robins and so on. Involve different groups of children in creating each collection to contribute to the display. (M1, 2, 3)

- Use a collection of Winter objects or pictures to reinforce positional language (see activity opposite). (M10)

KNOWLEDGE AND UNDERSTANDING OF THE WORLD

- On a walk look for signs that Winter is coming/has come. Show the children that some trees no longer have leaves. Look under stones for any remaining minibeasts. Look for birds and talk about ones which have flown away until the Spring. (K1, 2)

- In small groups go outside and ask children to pick out wintry scenes. Help the children to take photographs with a simple camera. (To maintain interest try to have them developed quickly!) (K1, 2, 9)

PHYSICAL DEVELOPMENT

- Pretend to be very cold. What can we do to get warm? Play an action game based on a traditional favourite: 'Simon says keep warm by..... running on the spot, clapping, stamping, blowing on hands, rubbing hands, rubbing toes' and so on. Encourage children to listen carefully - remember that if the instruction does not begin with 'Simon says', it should be ignored! (PD 1, 2, 3)

CREATIVE DEVELOPMENT

- Use runny paint to 'blow' winter trees. Show the children how to use a brush to place a large blob of runny paint at the bottom of a piece of paper. Provide each child with a straw and show them how to hold the straw at a low level, almost horizontal and blow the paint along. Changing the direction of the blowing will produce forks in knobbly branches as the Winter tree grows. (C5)

- Prepare pictures for a group Winter book. (C4)
- Use blue, white and black paint to make as many shades and tones as possible. Ask children to cover a 30 x 30cm piece of paper. When completed mount the squares together to form a Winter patchwork. (C1)

ACTIVITY: The object line

Learning opportunity: Developing and reinforcing the use of positional language within the context of Winter.

Early Learning Goal: Mathematical Development. Children will be able to use everyday words to describe position.

Resources: A collection of objects associated with Winter, such as a paper snowflake, a Christmas card, a plastic robin, a mitten and a toy snowman. A selection of Winter pictures mounted onto A4 cards (if possible one per child).

Organisation: Whole or part group, carpet-time activity.

Key vocabulary: Positional language such as 'next to', 'between', 'behind', 'in front of'.

WHAT TO DO:

Show the collection of Winter objects to the children. Talk about each one and make sure that the children are familiar with them.

Place the objects in a row. Use positional language as you talk about the line. 'The snowman is next to the robin. The card is between the snowflake and the mitten.' Use questions to encourage children to use the same language. 'What is next to the card?', 'What is between the snowflake and the snowman?'

Give each child a prepared card to hold and ask the children to stand in a row. Ask them to describe their positions. 'Who is next to the Christmas tree picture?' 'Who is between the reindeer and the bird table?'

To extend older or more able children, see if they can move into the right places 'Can you make the snowman be between the cracker and the woolly hat?' Ask the children to stand in a line, one behind the other, so you can include the language of 'in front of' and 'behind'. This can become quite demanding: 'If the snowman and the cracker change places, who will be next to the reindeer?'

ACTIVITY: A Winter book

Learning opportunity: Drawing and writing about their own ideas as children work together to make a book.

Early Learning Goal: Communication, Language and Literacy. Children will be able to use their phonic knowledge to write simple regular words and make phonetically plausible attempts at more complex words. They will use a pencil and hold it effectively to form recognisable letters, most of which are correctly formed.

Resources: A big book; blue sugar paper; chalks; hair-spray or commercial fixative spray; larger paper; card; staples or a needle and wool.

Organisation: Whole group introduction followed by small group work over the following days.

Key vocabulary: Book, cover, page, words, pictures, title, author.

WHAT TO DO:

Look at some big books. Show the children where the author's name is and talk about the cover. As you read the book draw attention to the illustrations.

Explain to the children that they are going to work together to make a big book of their own. Each child is going to draw a Winter picture which will become part of this special book.

Working in small groups, provide each child with a piece of A4 blue sugar paper and chalks with which to draw. Encourage children to talk about their experiences of Winter and to develop their own ideas about what to draw. Scribe a sentence at the bottom of each picture to record the ideas expressed. To prevent the chalks from smudging, take the pictures to a separate, well ventilated area away from the children, and spray with hair-spray or fixative.

Mount the pictures onto larger pieces of paper and staple or sew them together to make a book. Encourage children to help in preparing a front cover with title and group authorship.

DISPLAY

Display the Winter book, inviting children and group visitors to enjoy reading it.

Use the collection of objects from the maths activity to form the basis of a wintry interactive display to which children can contribute. Use labels to reinforce the positional language developed in the activity.

Week 2
WINTER FOODS

PERSONAL, SOCIAL AND EMOTIONAL DEVELOPMENT

- In Winter it can be difficult for birds to find enough food to eat. Discuss what birds eat and how children could help to feed the birds. (PS4)

- Set up a bird table with the children. Talk about the need to place it where cats cannot disturb the birds. Make a rota for children to take it in turns to change the water. Talk about the need to wash hands after touching the bird table. (PS8, 10)

COMMUNICATION, LANGUAGE AND LITERACY

- Encourage children to talk about Winter foods they enjoy, compiling favourite menus (see activity opposite). (L5, 16, 19)

- Set up the role play area as a Winter cafe. Provide a couple of low tables with table cloths, chairs, a counter, till, plastic crockery and cutlery, paper napkins and trays. Provide note pads and pencils to allow for emergent writing as orders are taken. Invite children's suggestions for a name for the cafe to be displayed. Use a blackboard and chalks to write a menu of 'Today's Specials' and prices. (L4, 16)

- Read or tell the story of 'The Enormous Turnip'. (L6)

MATHEMATICAL DEVELOPMENT

- Sort a selection of Winter vegetables according to size and shape. (M4, 12)

- Sing the song 'Five fat sausages cooking in a pan' (in *Okki-tokki-unga*). (M1, 2)

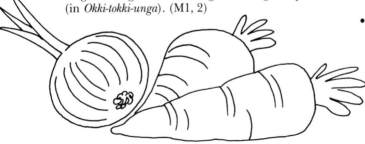

KNOWLEDGE AND UNDERSTANDING OF THE WORLD

- Make and use bird feeders (see activity opposite). (K5)

- Use a selection of Winter vegetables and paint to make vegetable prints. Compare the prints. Later in the week see whether children can match the prints to the vegetables. (K3)

- Bake bird biscuits (see activity opposite). (K5)

PHYSICAL DEVELOPMENT

- As you talk through the making of a Winter vegetable soup, encourage children to act out the processes. These might include growing and pulling the vegetables, peeling and chopping them, adding water and seasonings, stirring and pouring the soup, and enthusiastic tasting! (PD1)

- Make up a vegetable soup movement game. Designate areas of a large space using large pictures of vegetables. The centre of the space is the pot of soup. Call instructions for children to follow: 'Hop to the carrots', 'Creep to the cabbages' or 'Jump into the soup!'. (PD1, 2, 3)

CREATIVE DEVELOPMENT

- Make snowflake biscuits. Prepare an icing sugar mix which needs to be fairly wet but not too runny. Show children how to use a teaspoon to drop some of the mix onto a rich tea biscuit. Before the icing dries, show children how to use a dropper to allow just one or two drops of food colouring to fall onto the icing. Watch beautiful snow flake patterns appear as the colouring soaks into the icing. (C1)

- Talk about pasta as a warm winter food. Provide a variety of pasta shapes as a collage material. Talk about the shapes. Some are tubes, some look like wheels or shells, and so on. (Pasta can be coloured, by mixing with a little food colouring and drying in a gentle oven.) (C1)

ACTIVITY: Wintry menus

Learning opportunity: Making menus using simple words and pictures.

Early Learning Goal: Communication, Language and Literacy. Children will be able to attempt writing for various purposes...

Resources: A3-sized stiff paper folded into two; magazines with food pictures; scissors; crayons; felt pens; glue; pencils; sticky labels on which to write food names; an example of a real menu and, if possible, a child's version.

Organisation: Small group around a table.

Key vocabulary: A variety of words relating to food.

WHAT TO DO:

Talk to children about the kinds of things they like to eat on a cold, wintry day. What would their favourite lunch be? Why?

Show children an example of a real menu. Look at the way it is organised. Explain that they are going to make a wintry lunch menu. Some children may like to use pictures from magazines, some may wish to draw and others might copy words or ask for an adult to scribe for them. If words are written on sticky labels children can choose where to place them. Once made, the menus can be used as a stimulus for role play in a cafe.

ACTIVITY: Bird food and feeders

Learning opportunity: Talking about birds in the local environment. Using materials to make bird feeders.

Early Learning Goal: Knowledge and Understanding of the World. Children will be able to build and construct with a wide range of objects.

Resources: Foil trays; ingredients for pastry and bird cake (see below); plastic drinks bottles; milk cartons; strong string.

Organisation: Whole group discussion. For practical work, small groups. Over the week small groups will make a variety of feeders and bird food.

WHAT TO DO:

Show children pictures of birds which can be seen in the local environment. Talk about when and where children have seen the birds. Introduce the idea of regularly feeding birds. Show children a shop bought feeder. How does it work? Explain that during the week small groups will prepare different feeders and food for the birds.

Group 1: Bird cake

Mix together sunflower seeds, millet, currants, oatmeal, kitchen scraps and stale cake. Cover with melted fat. When slightly cooled press into round, foil dishes. Once cool the cake can be hung up as a 'feeding bell' or placed on a bird table. (NB Due to the severe nut allergies suffered by some children, the bird cake should not include peanuts.)

Group 2: Bird biscuits

Wholemeal pastry is excellent food for birds. Encourage children to describe the texture of the pastry as they roll it out. Use cutters of a variety of shapes to make the biscuits. Place the biscuits on a bird table. See which shapes the birds prefer.

Group 3: Feeders

Use milk cartons or plastic drinks bottles to make feeders. Although children will not be able to cut the holes for the feeders they should be encouraged to say where the hole should be made and to give reasons for their designs. Hang the feeders from a suitable nail or branch.

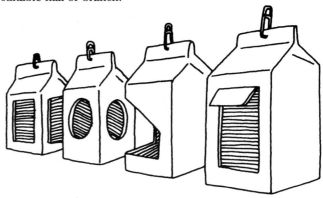

DISPLAY

On a table display a range of books and pictures of birds which children might see during the Winter. Each day put out a large piece of white paper on which children can draw/record birds they see on the bird table or feeders. Encourage children to notice what the birds are eating. At the end of two weeks make the sheets into a large book and share it with the group.

Week 3
WINTER WEATHER-SNOW

PERSONAL, SOCIAL AND EMOTIONAL DEVELOPMENT

- Talk about the need to handle other people's possessions with care. Talk about the snow storm display (see activity opposite) and using storms made by other children. (PS4)

- Read *Cuddly Dudley* by Jez Alborough (Walker) - a story about a penguin in the snow. Talk about brothers and sisters. How would the children feel if they were Dudley? (PS4, 12)

- Make a collection of picture books and pictures of animals which live in snowy areas. Talk to children about the animals. Make jigsaws from greetings cards picturing animals such as penguins and polar bears. Encourage children to work collaboratively to do the jigsaws. (PS8)

COMMUNICATION, LANGUAGE AND LITERACY

- Tell the children the story of 'The Snowman' by Raymond Briggs using a version which does not have text (for example, Puffin). Point out that there is no text in this book; the pictures tell the story all by themselves. (L4, 5)

- Make name labels for the snow storm display (see activity opposite). (L17, 19)

- Make a collection of 'cold' words (freeze, snow, ice, cold, sparkle, white, shimmer). Cut six-pointed snowflakes from white or silver paper and display a word on each. (L8)

MATHEMATICAL DEVELOPMENT

Provide each child with six snowmen holding hands cut from a piece of A4 folded white paper. Use the snowmen to develop:

- repeating pattern work - 'Colour alternate hats' (M8)

- number awareness - 'Give each snowman one nose, two eyes, and three buttons' (M1, 2)

- ideas of combination - 'Each snowman can have a red or blue hat, a green or yellow scarf, and an orange or carrot nose. Can you make each snowman different?' (M11)

- Make a dice-throwing 'beetle' game using snowmen. (M1, 2)

KNOWLEDGE AND UNDERSTANDING OF THE WORLD

- Use a cornflour modelling dough - see activity opposite. (K1)

PHYSICAL DEVELOPMENT

- Pretend to be a snowman melting on a hot day. (PD1)

- Use airflow balls or beanbags as imaginary snowballs. Practise catching and aiming. (PD6)

- Use white skittles or plastic bottles decorated as snowmen to practise aiming. (PD6)

CREATIVE DEVELOPMENT

- Make snowy 'spatter' pictures using white paint on black paper. For this you need brushes with short, firm bristles. (Old tooth brushes which have been sterilised are ideal.) Show the children how to dip the brush into the white paint and then to spatter paint onto the paper by either a sharp flicking action, or by running a finger towards themselves along the bristles. This takes practice and can be messy, but is highly enjoyable! Added interest can be achieved by laying templates onto the paper before splattering, and seeing the shape left as they are removed at the end of the activity. (C1)

- Make up a dance to the music from a video or audio tape of 'The Snowman'. (C4)

- Sing 'Jingle Bells'. (C4)

- Use desiccated coconut and/or glitter to make 'snowstorms' in see-through plastic bottles (see activity opposite). (C1)

ACTIVITY: Cornflower dough modelling

Learning opportunity: Exploring and manipulating a material as models are made.

Early Learning Goal: Knowledge and Understanding of the World. Children will be able to investigate...materials by using all their senses as appropriate.

Resources: Recipe:

2 cups salt

1 cup cornflour

1 cup water (warm)

Colouring (optional)

Oil (optional)

Mix ingredients in a pan over a low heat, stirring well until texture becomes firm.

Organisation: Small group (Caution: children with eczema on their hands should avoid skin contact with any form of dough which contains salt. Surgical gloves should be provided for these children.)

Key vocabulary: Mix, dough, shape, mould, model, bake.

WHAT TO DO:

Cornflour dough is used in just the same way as a traditional salt dough. It can be used to make models which are then dried slowly in a gentle oven for several hours. The models will then keep more or less indefinitely. Cornflour dough has the advantage of being much softer than ordinary salt dough and so is easier for small children to use. It is also very white, which in this case enables it to be used to make mock 'snow' models, but which also makes it satisfying to paint. However, because it is not as stiff as salt dough, it is best to make shapes and models which lie flat.

The dough can be painted once it is dry. Alternatively several batches can be made and a different colour added to each during the cooking process.

ACTIVITY: Snow storms

Learning opportunity: Exploring texture and space.

Early Learning Goal: Creative Development. Children will be able to explore texture...form and space...

Resources: Shop bought 'snow storm'; selection of safe snow-like materials such as desiccated coconut or glitter; old Christmas cards; clear plastic cups; sticky tape.

Organisation: Small group.

Key vocabulary: Shake, snowflake, fall, float, flutter, swirl.

WHAT TO DO:

Show children the shop bought 'snow storm'. Explain that they are going to make their own. Show them the snow materials. Do they remind the children of snow? How?

Half fill the cups with water. Put a spoonful of each snow material in each cup. Compare the way they float/fall. Gently swirl the cups. Talk about what happens.

Give each child a bottle. Ask them to cut a picture to be the scene for their snow storm. (The pictures can be stuck with tape around the bottle so that the picture can be seen through the bottle.)

Fill the bottles with water until they are three-quarters full. Invite each child to choose the material they want for their snow and put a dessertspoon in the bottle using a funnel. Screw the lid on tight - and shake!

DISPLAY

Cover a table with a white sheet. Place the snow storm bottles on the table. Add brief information labels which describe how the storms were made and invite friends and visitors to try them out.

Week 4

WINTER WEATHER- ICE

PERSONAL, SOCIAL AND EMOTIONAL DEVELOPMENT

- Talk about the need to be careful when out and about in icy weather. Why can it be dangerous to play at sliding on icy paths, especially near a road? Why should children never try to walk over frozen ponds? (PS12)

- Tell the children about people who help us when the weather is icy, such as the men who drive gritting lorries through the night so that people can travel safely in the morning. (PS3)

COMMUNICATION, LANGUAGE AND LITERACY

- Discuss children's experiences of freezing and melting. What is an ice lolly like when it is frozen? What happens when it melts? What frozen foods do children like to eat? Talk about favourite varieties of ice lollies and ice cream. What is it that makes these special? Where should frozen foods be kept? Refer back to Raymond Briggs' story of 'The Snowman'. Why did the snowman like to sit in the freezer? Reinforce relevant language: freeze, frozen, melt, melting, thaw, ice, water, solid and liquid. Encourage children to use descriptive language as they describe their own experiences and preferences. (L4, 5)

- Pass around an imaginary ice lolly. What does each child taste as they sample it? When does it begin to melt? (L7)

MATHEMATICAL DEVELOPMENT

- Use the ice cube counting rhyme (see activity opposite). (M1)

- Use lolly sticks to make patterns and shapes. Talk about the names of 2-D shapes as they are made, introducing the words triangle, square and oblong. Can children use lolly sticks to make a house shape? How many sticks do they need? (M9)

KNOWLEDGE AND UNDERSTANDING OF THE WORLD

- Talk about the need to wear shoes which grip well when it is icy. Make wax crayon rubbings of shoe soles. Compare the patterns. Which do children think have the best grip? (K1, 3)

- Make and melt coloured icebergs (see activity opposite). (K3)

PHYSICAL DEVELOPMENT

- Play a variation on the game of musical statues. Before playing music, each time give a different instruction about the shape into which the children are to 'freeze': a spiky shape, a round shape, a wide shape and so on. (PD1, 2)

- Use sliding apparatus, reinforcing language of slipping and sliding. Older or more able children will be able to slide in different ways, sitting, lying and so on. (PD6)

CREATIVE DEVELOPMENT

- Encourage children to think about words they could use to describe the appearance of trees on an icy or very frosty day. Provide children with large twig shapes pre-cut from dark paper and a selection of scraps of white, sparkly and shiny materials. Examples might include small strips of polythene, silver and white glitter, tinsel, foil, silver buttons or sequins. (C1)

- Use simple percussion instruments to talk about sounds which remind children of cold, icy weather. Use metallic instruments such as triangles, Indian bells and glockenspiels to compose a collaborative 'icy symphony'. (C2)

ACTIVITY: Ice cube rhyme

Learning opportunity: Using a counting rhyme for numbers five to one.

Early Learning Goal: Mathematical Development. Children will be able to say and use number names in order in familiar contexts.

Resources: None.

Organisation: Whole group sitting comfortably on the floor in a circle.

Key vocabulary: Freeze, frozen, melt, thaw, solid, liquid.

WHAT TO DO:

Talk about ice. What happens to it when it is left in a warm room? Check children understand the word 'melt'. Teach the group the rhyme with the actions:

Five cubes of freezing ice, (*Hold up five fingers*)

To make my drink cold and nice.

Now I drop one in my squash, (*Mime dropping one into a drink*)

Splash it goes, splish, splosh! (*Clap on 'splash', slide hands together for 'splish, splosh'*)

Slowly my cube melts away,

I've got four for another day. (*Hold up four fingers*)

Four cubes........

As children become more confident with the rhyme it can be changed to start with different numbers of cubes and by using two cubes in some of the drinks. This will encourage children to listen to the rhyme and to be observant as varying numbers of fingers are put down.

ACTIVITY: Make a giant iceberg

Learning opportunity: Observing, describing and recording changes as ice melts.

Early Learning Goal: Knowledge and Understanding of the World. Children will be able to look closely at similarities, differences, patterns and change.

Resources: Coloured water; large container; water tray.

Organisation: Small group.

Key vocabulary: Float, sink, smaller, bigger.

WHAT TO DO:

Colour some water using food colouring and freeze it in a large container. A plastic bucket or ice cream box is ideal for this purpose, large jelly moulds are even better.

Remove all the toys from the water tray and fill it with warm water. Explain to the children that you are going to put the frozen coloured 'iceberg' into the water. What do they think will happen? Will it float or sink?

Once the iceberg is in the water, encourage the children to watch carefully. What happens to the rest of the water in the tray? Where has this colour come from? How does the iceberg change?

Older or more able children will be able to record their observations in the form of drawings or paintings. Photographs are also a useful way of recording this experience for children to share later with friends.

DISPLAY

Display the decorated frosty branches with a variety of the words which children used to describe their ideas and experiences of icy weather.

Week 5

WINTER CLOTHES

PERSONAL, SOCIAL AND EMOTIONAL DEVELOPMENT

- Talk about the importance of looking after clothes properly, hanging coats on pegs, keeping shoes and socks in pairs and so on. Begin an 'I can.....' chart with each child. Challenges could include fastening shoes, putting on gloves, folding clothes and so on. Ensure all children are able to record some 'I cans'. (PS10)

- Have a winter dressing-up area. Provide small groups of children with a selection of Winter dressing-up clothes. Include mittens, scarves and hats. Who can dress themselves for an imaginary winter walk? (PS10)

COMMUNICATION, LANGUAGE AND LITERACY

- Talk about getting dressed for a Winter walk (see activity opposite). (L5)

- Encourage recognition of letter sounds by playing a game. 'I'm thinking of something to wear, and it begins with the sound....'. (L11)

MATHEMATICAL DEVELOPMENT

- Prepare a selection of pairs of gloves, mittens, boots, hats and scarves from coloured paper or card. Encourage children to sort them into pairs and to place them in groups according to colour and to shape. (M9)

- Use the gloves, mittens, boots, hats and scarves to make repeating patterns for the children to continue (for example, red glove, blue hat, green scarf, red glove.....). (M8)

- Provide each child with a photocopy of a scarf divided into about 12 sections. Encourage them to colour the scarves in repeating patterns. (M8)

KNOWLEDGE AND UNDERSTANDING OF THE WORLD

- Winter evenings are dark. Discuss what sorts of clothes are easy to see in the dark. Show children a range of reflective items which cyclists might wear to be easily visible. Provide each child with a paper armband to cover with reflective sequins or shiny scraps that would be easy to see at night. (K1, 4)

- Make a winter washing line (see activity below). (K1)

PHYSICAL DEVELOPMENT

- Hold a winter dressing-up race. (PD6, 2)

CREATIVE DEVELOPMENT

- Use mail order catalogues for children to cut up and select their favourite Winter outfit. Later, encourage children to paint self-portraits, modelling their choices. (C1)

ACTIVITY: Winter washing line

Learning opportunity: Describing and selecting materials.

Early Learning Goal: Knowledge and Understanding of the World. Children will be able to investigate materials using all of their senses as appropriate.

Resources: A variety of collage materials, wool scraps and textiles. Pre-cut shapes of Winter garments on thin card, about A4 in size.

Organisation: Small group.

Key vocabulary: Warm, thick, soft, fluffy, smooth, shiny.

WHAT TO DO:

Talk to the children about how they would describe their Winter clothes. What sorts of clothes are fluffy, soft, smooth, waterproof, shiny or warm?

Provide each child with a pre-cut shape and encourage them to decide what word would best describe that garment. A jumper might be 'fluffy' and a mackintosh 'smooth'. This word is going to be the theme of their individual collage.

Younger or less able children will need support and guidance as they select materials with which to cover their shape. Constantly reinforce the chosen adjective. Which of the materials on the table could be described in this way? Allow more able children to discriminate between materials, discussing their ideas as they make selections.

Display each completed collage garment, together with its relevant describing word, on a washing line display.

ACTIVITY: Getting dressed

Learning opportunity: Developing sequencing skills as an everyday experience is described.

Early Learning Goal: Communication, Language and Literacy. Children will be able to use talk to sequence...events.

Resources: Selection of outdoor Winter clothes.

Organisation: Whole group.

Key vocabulary: First, next, last, pull, push.

WHAT TO DO:

Use the process of getting ready for a Winter walk to develop sequencing skills. In what order are outdoor clothes put on? What would happen if we put clothes on in the wrong order?

Talk about how we pull a jumper over our heads, but push our arms into the sleeves. We pull up socks, but push our feet into boots. What other clothes do we push or pull? Encourage children to mime the actions as they think about putting on a variety of warm clothes.

DISPLAY

Make a display of Winter clothes labelled with names and describing words.

Week 6
WINTER FAIR

PERSONAL, SOCIAL AND EMOTIONAL DEVELOPMENT

- Talk about handling food. Why is it important to have very clean hands and equipment? (PS10, 12)

- Discuss how visitors to the group will be welcomed and cared for. (PS4, 8, 13)

- The fair may become a crowded event. Talk about safe behaviour. (PS12)

COMMUNICATION, LANGUAGE AND LITERACY

- Talk to the children about making posters to advertise the Winter fair. What information will people need? Scribe children's ideas onto large pieces of paper and then invite them to add decorations to make the posters attractive. (L16)

MATHEMATICAL DEVELOPMENT

- Use food preparation as an opportunity to develop understandings of shape and number. What shapes are the biscuits? How could we cut sandwiches into triangles, squares or oblongs? How many slices should each cake be cut into? (M9, 11)

- If you are going to charge for games or activities children will need individual adult support in handling money. However, it is helpful to talk to children about different coins, naming each one and describing its shape, colour and size. Do not expect young children to be ready to be able to count money or to understand about giving change. (M3, 9)

- Children can help you to prepare a 'Guess the number' game. This is a useful opportunity for children to encounter large numbers, as they help you, for example, to count sweets into a jar. (M11)

KNOWLEDGE AND UNDERSTANDING OF THE WORLD

- Make Winter vegetable soup (see activity below). (K3)

- Talk about the need to decorate the room, stalls and games for the Winter fair. Encourage children to contribute by making paper chains, crepe paper fringing, paper doilies or cut-out shapes to enhance the produce/game. Encourage children to ask questions about methods and materials they might use. (K6)

PHYSICAL DEVELOPMENT

- Practise games which will be played at the fair. (PD1, 2)

- The wintry day (see activity opposite). (PD1)

CREATIVE DEVELOPMENT

- Make a find-the-treasure game based on a snow scene. (C1, 4)

- Make a Winter wishing well from a large box and a bucket for people to donate loose change in at the fair. Decorate it with paper icicles and glitter. On the well write:

'As you wish, shut your eyes,

Hoping for a nice surprise.

It might come true or it might not

But it will help *.................. such a lot!'

* *insert name of group or charity*

(written by Jessica Ray aged 9) (C1)

ACTIVITY: Winter soup

Learning opportunity: Observing cooked and uncooked vegetables, cutting vegetables.

Early Learning Goal: Knowledge and Understanding of the World. Children will be able to look closely at differences, similarities...and change.

Resources: Large saucepan; range of vegetables; two chopping boards; knives which are sharp enough to cut raw vegetables but safe for children to use; two vegetable stock cubes per pan of soup.

Organisation: Pairs of children.

Key vocabulary: Slice, chop, cook, simmer, boil, raw, cooked.

WHAT TO DO:

Talk to children about soup. What does it taste like? Which flavours are children's favourites? Many people like to eat soup in Winter because it warms them up on a cold day.

Explain that the group is going to make soup for the Winter fair. Show children the vegetables they are going to use. Can they name them? What do they look like?

Help pairs of children under close supervision to chop a range of vegetables. Place the vegetable pieces in a large pan, cover with water and add two vegetable stock cubes. Save one piece of each vegetable for comparing with the cooked versions. Allow the soup to simmer for about half an hour. Cool to body temperature before serving to children. When cooked encourage children to compare the cooked vegetables with the raw pieces.

ACTIVITY: The wintry day

Learning opportunity: Listening and responding as a group in a role play context.

Early Learning Goal: Physical Development. Children will be able to move with confidence, imagination and in safety.

Resources: None.

Organisation: Whole group in a large space.

Key vocabulary: Stamp, rub, slip, slide, stride.

WHAT TO DO:

Start with the children sitting comfortably on the floor. Talk about a wintry day. It is cold but the sun is shining. Ask them to imagine they are going to go to play outside. First they must get ready. Talk through the process of putting on outdoor clothes (linking back to 'Winter clothes' week), with children acting out the movements.

Describe going through the door and into the cold air. Now it is time to warm up! Use actions such as stamping, rubbing hands, swinging arms, clapping or jumping on the spot.

Ask the children to test carefully to see if the ground is slippery. Start in thin snow which gradually gets deeper and deeper, with walking becoming very slow with high steps. Children step over cracks in the snow with long, definite strides.

Suddenly it starts to snow. The children skip about catching the snowflakes. They play in the snow, making snowballs and building snowmen. Now the snow begins to fall very heavily. Walking is a great effort, pushing against the wind and wiping snow from eyes. Fortunately the storm does not last long and the children are soon able to skip back to their door.

Feet are stamped to remove snow and boots are pulled off. Outdoor clothes are removed (and put away!) and the children settle down to enjoy a warm drink.

DISPLAY

From the ceiling hang long, dangling streamers of white, grey and pale blue crepe paper interspersed with silver tinsel. Cover windows with pieces of pale blue and grey tissue paper. The overall effect should be to turn the group's room into a dreamy, Winterland ready for the Winter fair.

On a table put out a collection of shiny materials, metal spoons and plastic mirrors for children to explore reflections. Arrange cushions on the floor with a box of Winter picture books.

BRINGING IT ALL TOGETHER

INTRODUCING THE WINTER FAIR

Talk to the children about the Winter fair and its purposes. You may decide to use this as a fund-raising opportunity for the group or a charity, or you may prefer simply to prepare and enjoy the fun.

Brainstorm together ideas for things to make and games to play. Talk about the jobs you'll need to do to prepare for the fair and also the things which will need to be done on the day. Explain that this is something which you are going to prepare together. Everyone will have something to do.

INVOLVING THE CHILDREN IN PREPARATIONS

The introductory discussion will have helped children to understand that there are plenty of jobs to be done.

GAMES TO MAKE:

- Pin (use Blu-tack rather than pins) the nose on the snowman.

- Guess the number of white bonbon sweets (snowballs) in a jar, or the number of sunflower seeds glued to a bird table picture.

- Throwing table tennis balls (snowballs) into a bucket.

- Guess the birthday of .... (a knitted snowman or toy penguin).

- Find-the-treasure game (Stick a flag on a snowy scene).

ITEMS WHICH COULD BE SOLD

- Mugs of winter soup (not too hot!) made by the children will be welcome on a cold day.

- Salt dough fridge magnets are easy for children to make. Show them how to roll out the salt dough and to cut shapes using small biscuit cutters.

Once the models are dry they can be painted by the children and varnished by adults. Small button magnets, to glue to the back of each shape, are inexpensive and can be purchased from most craft shops.

If a group helper grows herbs in pots or a garden, dry a few sprigs to make wintry 'herb bags' to flavour winter soups and stews. You'll need some pre-cut circles of cheap muslin or cotton, about ten centimetres across. Show children how to lay a selection of dried herb sprigs in the centre and then gather up the fabric to make a little bag. The neck can be tied with string.

ACCESSORIES

Encourage children to help you choose names for the stalls and games, and to decorate banners and notices. If the fair is for fun only, you could make winners' certificates for the games.

RESOURCES

RESOURCES TO COLLECT :

- Clear containers for making 'snow storms'.
- A commercially produced 'snow storm'.
- A cloth in blue or other wintry colours to use as a display background.
- A large plastic tub or jelly mould for making an 'iceberg'.
- Bird table (optional).
- Clean milk cartons to make bird feeders.
- Marbling inks and trays.
- Drinking straws.

EVERYDAY RESOURCES:

- Boxes, large and small for modelling.
- Papers and cards of different weights, colours and textures for example, sugar, corrugated card, silver and shiny papers and so on.
- Dry powder paints for mixing and mixed paints for covering large areas.
- Different sized paint brushes from household brushes to thin brushes for delicate work and a variety of paint mixing containers.
- A variety of drawing and colouring pencils, crayons, pastels, charcoals and so on.
- Additional decorative and finishing materials such as sequins, foils, glitter, tinsel, shiny wool and threads, beads, pieces of textiles, parcel ribbon.
- Table covers.
- Clear plastic cups and bottles.

STORIES

The Black Cat by Allan Ahlberg and Andre Amstutz (Little Mammoth).

Cuddly Dudley by Jez Alborough (Walker).

Winter Story by Jill Barklem (Collins).

Little Polar Bear by Hans de Beer (North South Books).

The Snow by John Burningham (Red Fox).

The Cross Rabbit by Nick Butterworth (Harper Collins).

The Winter Hedgehog by Ann and Reg Cartwright (Red Fox).

Jolly Snow by Jane Hissey (Red Fox).

Penguin Pete by Marcus Pfister (North South books).

The Cat in the Hat Comes Back by Dr Seuss (123 Beginner Book, Collins).

Little Penguin by Patrick Benson (Walker Books)

POETRY BOOKS

Early Years Poems and Rhymes compiled by Jill Bennett (Scholastic Ltd)

This Little Puffin by Elizabeth Matterson (Puffin).

Out and About by Shirley Hughes (Walker).

POSTERS

The Seasons - pack of four posters from *Practical Pre-School*.

SONGS

Harlequin 44 Songs Round the Year chosen by David Gadsby and Beatrice Harrop (A & C Black).

Okki-tokki-unga Action Songs for Children chosen by Beatrice Harrop, Linda Friend and David Gadsby (A & C Black).

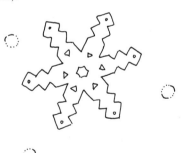

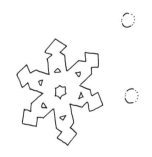

COLLECTING EVIDENCE OF CHILDREN'S LEARNING

Monitoring children's development is an important task. Keeping a record of children's achievements will help you to see progress and will draw attention to those who are having difficulties for some reason. If a child needs additional professional help, such as speech therapy, your records will provide valuable evidence.

Records should be the result of collaboration between group leaders, parents and carers. Parents should be made aware of your record keeping policies when their child joins your group. Show them the type of records you are keeping and make sure they understand that they have an opportunity to contribute. As a general rule, your records should form an open document. Any parent should have access to records relating to his or her child. Take regular opportunities to talk to parents about children's progress. If you have formal discussions regarding children about whom you have particular concerns, a dated record of the main points should be kept.

KEEPING IT MANAGEABLE

Records should be helpful in informing group leaders, adult helpers and parents and always be for the benefit of the child. However, keeping records of every aspect of each child's development can become a difficult task. The sample shown will help to keep records manageable and useful. The golden rule is to keep them simple.

Observations will basically fall into three categories:

- **Spontaneous records:**

Sometimes you will want to make a note of observations as they happen, for example, a child is heard counting cars accurately during a play activity, or is seen to play collaboratively for the first time.

- **Planned observations:**

Sometimes you will plan to make observations of children's developing skills in their everyday activities. Using the learning opportunity identified for an activity will help you to make appropriate judgements about children's capabilities and to record them systematically.

To collect information:

- talk to children about their activities and listen to their responses;

- listen to children talking to each other;

- observe children's work such as early writing, drawings, paintings and 3D models. (Keeping photocopies or photographs is sometimes useful.)

Sometimes you may wish to set up 'one off' activities for the purposes of monitoring development. Some groups, for example, ask children to make a drawing of themselves at the beginning of each term to record their progressing skills in both co-ordination and observation. Do not attempt to make records following every activity!

- **Reflective observations:**

It is useful to spend regular time reflecting on the progress of a few children (about four each week). Aim to make some brief comments about each child every half term.

INFORMING YOUR PLANNING

Collecting evidence about children's progress is time consuming and it is important that it is useful. When you are planning, use the information you have collected to help you to decide what learning opportunities you need to provide next for children. For example, a child who has poor pencil or brush control will benefit from more play with dough or construction toys to build the strength of hand muscles.

Example of recording chart

Name: Jonathan Green		D.O.B. 15.7.97		Date of entry: 13.9.00	
Term	**Personal, Social and Emotional Development**	**Communication, Language and Literacy**	**Mathematical Development**	**Knowledge and Understanding of the World**	**Physical Development**	**Creative Development**
ONE	Quickly and independently dresses for outdoor play. Eager to help peers with shoes etc. Can tie loose bow. 20.1.01 EMH	Enjoying listening to stories. Independently wrote 'Jon' for the group 'big book' 20.1.01 EHL	Is able to say numbers to ten and to count accurately five objects. Can recognise and and complete simple repeating patterns. 5.3.01 SJS	Very keen to observe melting ice. Good use of vocabulary for describing observations. 16.2.01 LSS	Finds it hard to balance on one leg. Enjoys aiming at skittles. Starting to control speed and direction of ball. 16.2.01 AC	Enjoys gluing and cutting. Made a wonderful Winter colage. 20.3.01 LSS
TWO						
THREE						

SKILLS OVERVIEW OF SIX WEEK PLAN

Week	Topic focus	Personal and Social and Emotional Development	Communication Language and Literacy	Mathematical Development	Knowledge and Understanding of the World	Physical Development	Creative Development
1	Detecting Winter	Appreciating the environment Being sensitive to others	Collaborative early writing Appreciating books	Counting Developing positional language	Observing Recording	Moving imaginatively Increasing control	Handling materials Painting
2	Winter foods	Treating living things with care and concern	Listening Role play Talking Early writing	Sorting Number awareness	Comparing Observing Making	Moving imaginatively	Using a variety of materials Glueing
3	Winter weather - Snow	Being sensitive to others Working collaboratively	Discussing Writing Enjoying stories and poems	Counting Making patterns	Comparing Observing	Imaginative movement Aiming	Handling materials Singing Dancing
4	Winter weather - Ice	Safety awareness	Language development	Counting Shape and pattern	Observing Comparing	Moving with imagination and control	Working with a variety of materials Using instruments
5	Winter clothes	Looking after ourselves	Discussing Recognising sounds	Sorting Making patterns	Observing Comparing	Fine motor skill development	Cutting and painting
6	Winter fair	Caring for others Safety and hygiene awareness	Knowing that words and pictures carry meaning Early writing	Recognising shapes Number	Comparing Observing Questioning	Moving with control	Making for a purpose

HOME LINKS

The theme of Winter lends itself to useful links with children's homes and families. Through working together children and adults gain respect for each other and build comfortable and confident relationships.

ESTABLISHING PARTNERSHIPS

- Keep parents informed about the topic of Winter, and the themes for each week. By understanding the work of the group, parents will enjoy the involvement of contributing ideas, time and resources.

- Photocopy the Parent's page for each child to take home. This will give parents additional information which will enable them to support the topic through shared activities, encouraging children to be aware of seasonal changes in their environment.

- Invite friends, carers and families to attend the Winter fair.

GROUP VISITORS

- Invite adults known to the children to come and talk to the children about childhood memories of Winter.

- Invite parents and friends to tell the children about their knowledge or experience of a variety of Winter traditions and celebrations.

RESOURCE REQUESTS

- Shiny scraps and old greetings cards will be useful materials to collect.

THE WINTER FAIR

- Help will be needed in supporting children as they make their games. At the event it will be helpful to have additional adult helpers to assist children as they take charge of their games and stalls.